I LOVE YOU
DADDY

Written by Roger Carlson

Illustrated by Elena Bogatireva

This book is dedicated to the loveliest lady in my life and my reason for throwing my feet over the bed every morning. Mariana, you inspire me to be my best.

Hi! My name is Mariana.

1

This is my dog Bella.

This is my daddy, Roger.

Daddy loves me a whole bunch. However, sometimes I do things that make me wonder why he loves me so much. That is what this book is about.

Daddy says that he has seven nieces and seven nephews.
Wow that means I have fourteen cousins.

For many years, Daddy dreamed of having a little girl just like me.
One day it happened. He said it was the happiest day of his life.

This story begins when I was seven months old. That is when I was adopted. Daddy told me when he held me for the first time he never wanted to let me go. I reached up and put my hand on his face. I am sure I could already feel his love. He told me he cried tears of joy the rest of the day. Daddy has been holding me and loving me ever since. I am such a lucky little girl. Daddy tells me he is the lucky one.

Daddy took a picture of our hands when I was a year old. My whole hand fit into the palm of his hand. I was so-o-o-o tiny! Babies can't take care of themselves. I know Daddy took good care of me.

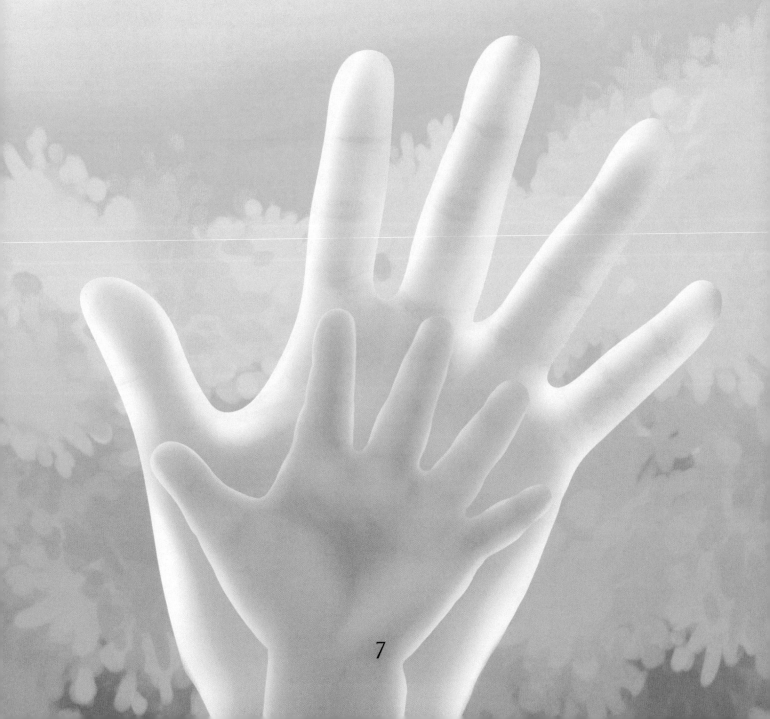

Daddy told me when I was a baby he changed a lot of diapers. Changing diapers is a messy job. Sometimes changing diapers is really messy. Sometimes it is **really, really** messy. Like the time I pushed the diaper full of ooey gooey poopy off the changing table. It fell onto his slipper. Ick!! He told me he just smiled and finished cleaning me up. Daddy is so patient.

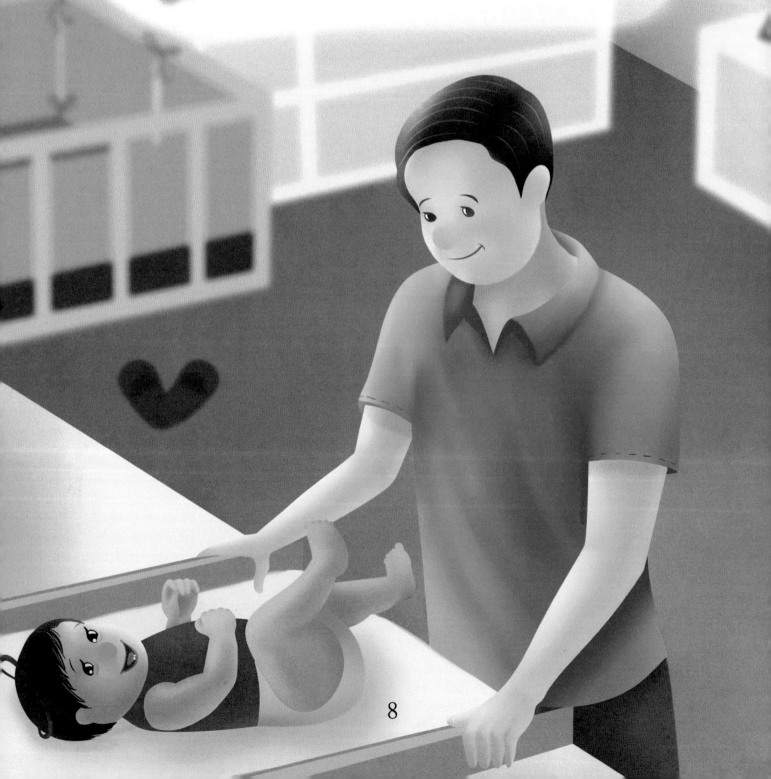

Daddy told me a story. When I was two years old, he was running late for work. He says being a parent is stressful sometimes. This morning I was not cooperating. I tossed the plate of eggs off the high chair, and it landed in his lap. Oops! I would have been mad if I was Daddy! He used his stern voice when he talked to me about my behavior. He cleaned up the mess and made me a new breakfast. This time I ate it all. He changed his clothes and off we went.

9

When I was three, I was chasing Bella around at the park, and I went potty in my pants. I really thought Daddy would be mad at me. He assured me that accidents happen. He had extra clothes in the car and helped me change. When we got into the car, he looked into the mirror and said, "I love you Mariana."

10

Daddy bought me a new dress. I couldn't wait to wear it. The only problem was I also wanted to paint. I did both. I got paint all over my face, the wall and even my new dress. When Daddy saw the mess, he said it wasn't my best decision. He said I need to paint in my old clothes next time. He talked to me about taking responsibility for my things. I helped him clean up the mess. Then he gave me a hug and said, "I love you."

11

I just turned four years old and Daddy bought me my very own big girl bed. That was s-o-o-o cool. Daddy says I am growing up way too fast. The first night I slept on it, I rolled off and fell to the floor. Daddy heard the thud and came running in. He asked if I was ok and held me until I stopped crying.

The next day Daddy installed a bed rail. I never fell off again. Daddy says it is his job to keep me safe.

I love to take bubble baths. I really like all the suds. One time, the suds spilled over the side of the tub and onto the floor. Daddy heard me giggling and splashing. He walked in and saw the slippery mess. Gasp! He just shook his head and laughed.

After my bath, I put on my p.j.'s and hopped into bed. He read me a story like he does every night. Before he turned off the light, he told me that he loved me. In the morning the bathroom was clean.

15

When I was five, I started to hide candy in my room. Sometimes I hide it under the bed. Sometimes I hide it at the back of my drawer, and sometimes I hide it under my mattress. When I have friends over, we sneak and eat my hidden candy. One time Daddy found my hiding place and took away all my candy. He said, "Too much candy is not good for you." Psst, I still hide candy when I get it. Ha Ha!

I enjoy playing board games with Daddy. He has taught me that sometimes you win and sometimes you lose. He says it is very important to be nice even when someone else wins. That can be hard sometimes.

I sit in the back seat of the car because I am still too young to sit in the front. When we go on a trip, we like to play games with our imaginations. One time, we pretended that we were a big fish in the ocean. We imagined that we could see lots of other fish swimming around us. We even saw a big scary shark. Yikes!

Another time, we imagined we were driving through a dusty desert. We saw a big, weird-looking flying dinosaur. He chased us. I am glad we got away.

19

When I was six years old, Daddy took me swimming at a friend's house. I was having so much fun playing that when it was time to go, I would not get out of the pool.

After a couple of minutes, Daddy waved goodbye and walked away. I ran after him. I did not want him to leave without me. Later, Daddy said I need to listen, be respectful, and obey.

At my seventh birthday party, my daddy planned some fun games. One of the games was an egg race with spoons. We used real uncooked eggs.

When we were finished with the egg race, we had a raw egg fight. Instead of being upset my daddy joined in. Most of the eggs landed on the ground, but I ran up behind my daddy and threw one at him. It landed on his leg and exploded. The yellow yoke ran down his leg. After the party we were cleaning up. Daddy told me he has parties so I can have good memories with friends. I have to say, I like to have friends.

I really enjoy playing basketball. Daddy is my basketball coach. One day when I was eight, we had a game. I did not score any points for the team. I was a little down about it. Daddy gave me a high-five at the end of the game. It made me feel better.

24

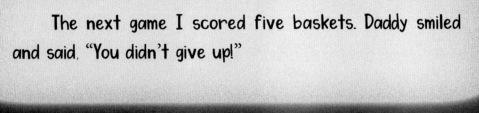

The next game I scored five baskets. Daddy smiled and said, "You didn't give up!"

Sometimes, there are bullies at school. Daddy tells me if someone bullies me or someone else, ask them to stop. Then tell mom or dad and a teacher.

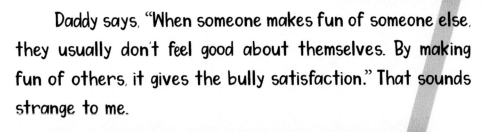

Daddy says, "When someone makes fun of someone else, they usually don't feel good about themselves. By making fun of others, it gives the bully satisfaction." That sounds strange to me.

Daddy says, "Let the bullies' words bounce off you like a basketball bounces off the backboard." He says, "Never bully anyone. Be kind to others, even the bullies."

I have a lot of friends. My daddy teaches me that it does not matter what color skin you have, or where you are from, you should love everyone the same. I hope everyone has someone who loves them.

Daddy taught me to make my bed in the morning. He said he learned that from Grandma. He taught me that making my bed is the first of many accomplishments for the day. It will also make me feel good to come home to a made bed.

I remember one time I was mad at my daddy for some reason. He asked me to give him a hug. When I told him, "No" he replied, "It's ok, your hugs are your hugs. You can give them when and to whom you want." He said, "I love you, Mariana, even when you are unhappy with me. I will always love you."

31

Daddy says spending time together is much better than getting presents. One time, Daddy told me he had lots to do. I really wanted to tell him about my day. I asked him if we could talk. Instead of rushing, we went for a long walk and talked the whole time. It was just Daddy and I. It was great.

Every year we go camping. Daddy says he really wants me to enjoy nature. I like to sit around the campfire and listen to the snap, crackle and pop. It is awesome.

Daddy taught me to pray before I fall asleep each night. I ask God to bless my mommy, daddy, and everyone else in the world. I also ask God to help me be kind and loving.

34

Daddy says, "One day Mariana, you will be on your own. This is why your mother and I want to teach you what you need to know today… for tomorrow."

Forgive

Loving others

Faith

Working hard

Helping those less fortunate

Patience

Respect

Humor

Loving yourself

Discipline

Imagination

Consideration

Courage

Honesty

Kindness

Perseverance

Compassion

Generosity

Giving and receiving love

But for now, I am just going to enjoy being a kid and play with my slime. Hey, I have a story to tell you about what happened last summer with my slime. Wait, that will have to be told another day... in another book.

36

ACTIVITY QUESTIONS TO STORY PAGES

PAGE	QUESTIONS
6	What does it mean to be adopted? Do you know anyone who is adopted?
7	What does your mom or dad do that makes you feel loved?
8	What is your favorite story that your mom or dad told you about when you were a baby?
9	What is the worst mess you have made so far? How do you help your parents clean up your messes?
10	Do you have a dog? What do like to do with your dog?
11	What do you like about art? What art projects do you like to do with your parents?
13	What do your parents do that makes you feel safe?
14	Do you like to take a bath? What games do you play when you take a bath?
15	Do one of your parents read to you each day? Do you read every day? What is your special book?
16	Do you ever hide stuff in your room? What stuff have you hidden in your room?
17	What board games do you like best and why? How do you feel when you lose a game?
18	What kind of games do you play in the car with your mom and dad?
19	What do you think it would be like to live with the dinosaurs?
20	Do you know how to swim? Where do you like to go swimming? Who usually goes with you?
21	What does the word respect mean? How do you show respect to adults? When is a time that you were not respectful to your mom or dad? How did you feel?
22	What did you do at your last birthday party?
24	What sports do you like to play?
25	Do you remember when you won a game? How did winning make you feel?
26	What does the word "bully" mean?
27	Have you ever been bullied? How did you feel when you were bullied?
28	Have you ever bullied anyone? If you have, how do you think the person felt?
30	Why are chores important? What do you like to help your parents do around the house?
31	Are you ever mad at your parents? What happened that made you mad?
32	If you have a choice between getting a present or spending special times with parents, which would you choose? What kinds of things have you done with mom or dad that you enjoyed?
33	What do you think would be fun about camping?
36	Do you enjoy making slime? What is your favorite kind of slime? If you really like slime you should have your mom or dad buy Daddys next book that is titled: The Day Slime took over the house. Wouldn't that be scary?

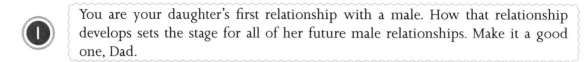

REMINDERS FOR DADS WITH DAUGHTERS

1 You are your daughter's first relationship with a male. How that relationship develops sets the stage for all of her future male relationships. Make it a good one, Dad.

2 Your daughter will, more than likely, find someone to marry whom she believes will treat her children the way you treated her. If you think about that carefully, it is a huge responsibility. Give her an example of what it means to be a great dad. You should want your future grandkids to have a great dad as well.

3 Quality time with your children is priceless. Be aware that the "stuff" you give to your children does not always contribute to their well-being.

4 Kids are only kids once. Cherish every memory. Remember, there are no do-overs.

5 Read to your children every night. When they can read on their own, take turns reading to each other.

6 Make sure your children have age appropriate chores. Doing chores together provides an opportunity to bond.

7 For the days your children are with you, tell them you love them every morning and every night before they go to bed. Make it a goal to kiss them at least once a day.

8 Remember, you are a parent before you are a friend. Do not be afraid to say "no."

9 Pick a date each year to reflect with your co-parent on the past year. Write down your reflections in a journal. What do each of you believe you did well? What can you improve? The next year, take the journal out and discuss the past and plan for the future.

10 Education is a vital part of your children's development. Stay active in your children's school life. Be aware of what your children are learning.

11 Make your home a welcoming place. Get to know your children's friends and their parents.

12 Teach your children that diversity is a beautiful thing.

13 Being a parent is rewarding, but it is also difficult at times. Develop a strong support network.

14 Keep a bubble of protection around your children without being over protective. Be careful not to involve your children in your adult conversations. Do not allow them to be in the middle of parental disputes.

REMINDERS FOR DADS WITH DAUGHTERS

15 Do not confuse workaholism for good work ethic. If you find yourself working too much, consider what you might be avoiding.

16 Remember, no parent says or does the right thing all the time. Do not be afraid to ask for professional help if necessary.

17 Remember the best thing you can do for your child is to take care of yourself. This includes your mind, body, and spirit.

18 Avoid pushing your child into an activity because it is something you wish you could have done. Likewise, avoid pushing your child into an activity because you did it. Know the difference between encouraging and pushing.

19 Set aside time alone with your spouse or significant other that does not involve discussing your children. Children thrive when they see that they are not the only focus of their parents' lives.

20 When things get difficult, as they do for every parent, be strong in knowing that you have this unique and awesome responsibility.

21 If you are a parent with grown children and have regrets about not being the parent you could have been, leave the regrets behind. You cannot change the past. Forgive yourself for the mistakes you made.

22 Most importantly, enjoy being a parent.

COMING SOON

Follow up with Mariana in the upcoming book series.

The day Slime took over the house

Mariana Wayback Book-Washington's Riddles

Precious Moments with Dick and Jane

The day Slime took over the neighborhood

For more inspirational books visit our web site
www.marianapublishing.com

Find us on:

SPECIAL THANKS

Through an act of providence, Roger crossed paths with a psychologist by the name of Roseann Woodka, PhD, and she has become a good friend and inspiration. As his editor, Roseann's advice has been crucial in the development of this book.

ABOUT THE AUTHOR

ROGER CARLSON holds a Bachelor's degree in Education and an MBA, both from Indiana University. In addition, he has an undergraduate degree in Electrical Engineering Technology from Purdue. During his career, Roger has worked as a math teacher and a mechanical and electrical engineer.

A few years ago, Roger had a dream of writing a book about his experiences with his beautiful little girl. He entertained this idea when she was five years old. Over the next couple of years, he began to write down some of the memories he had made with his daughter. His next task was to begin looking for an illustrator. After an extensive search through several great illustrators, he finally found the right one. They began working together to create the best illustrations they could. After several years, the final page was written and illustrated. Roger hopes you enjoyed reading this book and will look for other inspirational books at www.marianapublishing.com and on Amazon.

ISBN: 978-1-64510-000-3 hardback

ISBN: 978-1-64510-001-0 (IngramSpark)

ISBN: 978-1-64510-002-7 (Amazon)

ISBN: 978-1-64510-003-4 (Print on Demand)

ISBN: 978-1-64510-004-1 (Kindle ebook)

First Published in 2019

Printed in the USA

Made in the USA
Middletown, DE
15 December 2019